2-

WHAT NATURE KNOWS

poems & meditations

CHRISSA VENTRELLE

FROM a FRIEND Project

First published by the From a Friend Project, 2021

Illustrations by Hillary Waters Fayle
Book design by Shanna Compton

Printed in Canada

 This book is printed on paper certified to
the environmental and social standards
of the Forest Stewardship Council™ (FSC®)

ISBN: 978-0-578-91096-3 (hardcover)
ISBN: 978-0-578-91097-0 (paperback)

For more information, please visit
www.ChrissaVentrelle.com

To Dan,
Drew, Brooke, and Ryan

NATURE AS GUIDE

It's Like This

7

LET'S . . .

An Invitation for Togetherness

62

NATURE AS GUIDE

It's Like This

A hibiscus waits
for dawn
to greet her
on the other side
of dark. She's
poised for a revival
when the light arrives,
ready to fan out
her ruffled, radiant self,
veiling nothing,
her vibrancy
unabashedly
vivid and
exposed.

In awe of humble moss
with the agency
to cover granite's
deepest crevice,
to blanket oak's
fallen branch,
to coax green from
tundra's frozen land.

With no roots
as birthright,
her tiny leaves splay
in receptive delight,
collecting nutrients
from the air around,
fueled simply by mist or fog.

When the air hangs
thick with toxins,
the moss absorbs
this darkness too,
which leaves her sick and
withered. But move
her to a healthy place
and she revives,
verve renewed.

Two beech trees,
forest kin

from saplings,
slow to grow

yet long to live,
their silvery bark

tattooed with markings
etched over ages,

growing sturdy
side by side,

arranging their
winter crowns

so both may
share the sun.

Below, roots
intertwine and nutrients

flow between them,
especially in times

of stress. When
one suffers, the other

aches, when one thrives
the other flourishes too.

From afar
honey is honey,
all sweet and gold,
but up close
this honey,
that honey,
this honey,
each its own,
its hue a range
from morning sun
to evening amber,
its flavor as varied as
spicy and fruity.

Each drop's a portrait
of a nectar feast:
alfalfa's purple blooms,
the flushed flowers
of fireweed,
white fused petals
of a blueberry bush,
all adding to the
the hive's unique honey,
every drop telling
its own origin story.

Hard frost cloaks
the olive tree in white,
blighting branches, forcing
silvery leaves to shed.

It looks bleak from above,
but beneath the frozen earth,
the tree's ancient rootstock
lies poised to regenerate.

It's a quiet resurrection
born from happenings
unseen, unheard
in the dark soil.

Come spring, new
slender shoots emerge,
stretching upward
to hug the trunk's base.

Like this, she outlives war and pests,
drought and rime, her branches
outstretched in peaceful greeting,
resilient as the long arms of time.

Proximity to a miracle
doesn't make it less divine—
just paddle to the backwater's
wild edge where a mangrove seed
grows long as a falcon's feather
then drops into the brackish water
and bobs across
the wide, bossy ocean until
it maroons in foreign sand.

The brave voyage
is cause enough
for awe, but then
seed sets to serve as tree,
inviting sand to settle
round its interlaced roots,
building new ground where
there was none,
a hero stabilizing the shore,
buffering land from storm,
filtering salt through roots,
and offering cover to countless
creatures of land and sky and sea.

Born in the shallow backwaters
of a no-name estuary,
a study in the miraculous
camouflaged by the familiar.

A sculpture is born
from translucent
marble, its light
freed by an artist
called to shape
its placid surface.

Before the sculpture,
marble forms
from humble limestone,
forever altered
by the forces of
heat and pressure.

Before the marble,
limestone emerges
from a stew
of marine sediment,
algae, coral, shells,
gathering and compacting,
gathering and compacting,
until rock forms.

Tossed among the
marine sediment lie

the shells of a mussel
once affixed to rock,
quietly serving by
commanding its valves
to open and close,
open and close,
its rhythmic motion turning
murky water clear.

From mollusk to
limestone to
marble to
sculpture,
an unpredicted passage,
each iteration vital to the next.

When clouds
gather tight and
coat the sky
gray, heralding
the rain to paint
the parched desert
floor, the thirsty
succulent absorbs
the moisture,
each drop essential
to replenish her
wizened leaves.

Like a squirrel
caching acorns,
she stores
extra water
in her core,
sustenance
for the next
dry spell, when
she will extract
these inner
reserves, aware
her planning will

leave her stressed
but not damaged,
grateful to greet
the next rainfall.

The hummingbird knows
nature rewards the creative,
as she crafts a nest
smaller than a daffodil's cup,
formed from grass and fibers
woven tight with spiders' silk,
shingled with seeds and lichen,
engineered to stretch as her
chicks grow. An efficient home,
made from nature's bounty
with no tools, no currency,
a haven born
from her inspired design.

A lightning strike
stuns the night sky
as dark surrenders

to momentary bright,
a single bolt
enough

to bring havoc
on orbital order
where dusk

leads to dark
and dark to dawn
in a diurnal loop

of light. The
white-hot flash
disrupts this cycle

with conviction,
its luminosity
masking

its true girth,
no thicker
than a twig.

In a stand of Douglas fir
amidst a forest dark and dense,

the evergreen prunes herself,
favoring branches that pulse

with vitality close to the light,
while withholding nutrients

from limbs taking more than
they give. It's this paring down,

rewarding what gives energy
and shedding what doesn't,

that enables the fir
to grow for centuries.

To self-prune is to renew.

Salt water, fresh water,
both born from
hydrogen and oxygen
but unique in weight
and temperature,
salinity and flow,
travel from the river,
travel from the sea,
to meet in the estuary,
sometimes flowing
one atop the other
in opposing directions,
but more often mixed
by turbulence to create
a wondrous brew
of brackish water
teeming with rich nutrients,
all precious and productive.
It's like this, too, when
holding space
for differing views.

A pear won't fully
ripen on a tree.
It must separate first
from its branch
before maturing
into the sweet
and slightly gritty
fruit of rolling
bumps and curves.

Pull too soon
and the pear
clings to the limb
in protest.
When ready, though,
a gentle tug
is all it needs
to part from its
source, now free
to wholly ripen,
its sweetness rising
day by day.

It's like this.

A lone red feather
orphaned by
a cardinal's wing
disrupts a white
blanket of snow,
a spot of chaos
amidst uniformity,
a single plume
of fiery pigment
set upon
a smooth canvas,
both made
more brilliant
by the intersection
of bold and blank.

Trees start low
then stretch high.
That's the order
of the universe—
or so it's thought—
until the banyan tree
reminds us there is
always another
way to grow.

Its aerial roots
hang first
from lofty branches,
then string
down the trunk
like nautical rope,
maturing from
gangly to thick
until each stands
as its own sturdy pillar
to bear the load
of the banyan's
weighty canopy.

Young roots mimic
this downward

dance, and over
generations
the tree covers
acres, growing
top to bottom,
top to bottom,
ignoring all the rules.

We honor wheat
as the staff of life,
milled to flour, mixed
and proofed, then
baked to bread,
its yeasty
scent a signal
of safekeeping.

But it's all impossible
without service
from the chaff, wheat's
unsung protector
from grain mites
and sawflies and frost
and drought.

After threshing the chaff
from the wheat,
the husk's duty
seems complete
but its purpose
stretches further—
as roofing for shelter,
fuel for fire,

fodder for flock,
or ground cover to stop
weeds from taking root.

Bamboo
is botany's cheetah,
earth's fastest-growing plant,
with shoots that can
stretch an arm's length
between the span of
dawn and dusk.

But rewind
to bamboo's first spring
and discover
just a tender stalk
or two. The spring
that follows
coaxes only a
few sprouts more.

Another year passes and
then the culms explode.
Each new season after
the canes stretch
taller and wider,
taller and wider
than those that came
before. New ideas
spread like this too.

Most birds sing
as ribbons of light
stretch across
the horizon,
but the whip-poor-will
serenades the moon,
a steady carol
breaking the still night.

And most owls
sleep by day,
then call under cover
of dark, but not the
burrowing owl
whose golden
eyes stay alert
with the sun.

Each creature
honoring her
true nature,
adapting in
her own way.

It's good fortune
for a seedling
swept across
the desert floor
to sprout beneath
the canopy
of a plant
deep-rooted there.

The elder gives
shelter from heat
and harm while
nature rewards
her kindness
with bonus blooms,
dressing her
with more flowers
than neighbors
with no seedlings
in their care.

Seedling
and caregiver
flourish together
as generosity

grows
generosity.

Each year the fig tree
bears two crops—

the first early in
the season, too acidic

and small. So she takes
a short rest, then

tries once more, this time
producing loads

of plump and hearty
fruit. She provides

nourishment this way
for ten millennia,

an agent of abundance
born from persistence.

When the wind howls
don't assume she's angry—

it's just her way
of passing through.

It's noisy work
to weave

through all that
blocks her path

as she splits herself
to skirt around

an object then pulls
together again,

this motion causing her
to whistle high

or moan low,
acoustic byproducts

of moving
with focus

to her next
destination.

A date palm seed
lies dormant, tucked
among fragments
of ancient clay vessels
hidden thousands of years
by layer upon layer
of sediment,
deep and dark,
until the search
for Biblical treasures
leads human hands
to unearth it,
returning it to light
then nurturing it
with soil, sun, and water,
until the seed replies by
sprouting upward,
now freed to fill a longing
held in waiting
for two millennia.

Whether along a country road
or across the globe,
the latitude changes,
the soil varies,
the climate differs,
but the blackberry bramble
always finds a way to grow,
trusting the warmth
of the sun to turn
its sour fruit sweet.

A nest is a nest is a nest
for those who skip on by,
but wonder awaits
those who stop to see.

For the quail, home
is a shallow depression
or even an abandoned nest,
a free and easy place of refuge.

For the eagle, a cavernous
basket of branches sits
high above the fray, sturdy
for return year after year.

The hummingbird's nest
starts with tiny fibers woven tight
with spiders' silk, all designed
to stretch with growing chicks.

To overlook the singularity
of each is to miss
the builder's soul, heeding
her primal need for home.

The agave blooms,
pushing flowers skyward
just once a generation,

trumpeting
her end of life
and celebrating

her impact yet to come.
Her parts are then
dried or roasted or mashed

for food, then more—
leaves become a thatch for homes,
her juice a heady drink,

her nectar a sweetener,
her thorn a sewing needle,
her fiber cord for rope,

her stalk a maker of music.
A legacy of generosity,
even in the desert.

The slow-growing yew,
a master of regeneration,
survives century after century
by pushing fresh buds
from haggard wood
that appears long lifeless
and decayed, then drops
new roots where
old branches droop and
kiss the ground,
stamping its legacy
with fresh green needles
pointing skyward.

The willow's
long-armed branches
dip into the quiet pond,
her grace gift enough.
Then the discovery:
her simple bark,
a lifesaving soother
of pain, the essence of
aspirin. As a breeze rises,
this unassuming giver
of miracles sways her
lanky limbs and sets
her leaves aflutter.

The days scrunch small,
the nights stretch long,
and a frozen crust coats the land.
But the holly bush beams brightly,
alight with crimson berries
and shiny leaves,
its sprigs a beacon
of coming celebration.

While most woodland life
sits still in submission
to the frosty air and
punishing winds,
the holly bush thickens
her leaves and gives them
a warm, waxy coat to wear,
then shares her fruit
with deer and squirrel and
robin and waxwing,
a welcome feast in the
barren winter.

The desert is kindest
to those with nimble spirits,
who relax into
the unblemished blue
skies and unmarred soil,
who accept
her barren scape with
heat unrelenting and
exposure unforgiving.

She favors those
who rest when weary,
drink when parched, let
the dry air heal wounds,
and exhale with the
rising sun and moon.

Speckles on a robin's egg,
veins on a maple leaf's back,
crystal formations on a snowflake,
never twice the same.

Each a study
of the natural and unbound
that never seeks
forgiveness for singularity,
but trumpets the wonder
born from originality.

The green seeds
of a cottonwood tree
drift on breezes while
wrapped in fleecy fibers
that mimic snow in June.

Traveling like pilgrims,
these little puffs
flit far and farther
from their birth tree,
undeterred by
fences and borders.

Millions of seeds
coat the prairies
in whispery fluff,
their presence
softening the landscape,
if only for a bit.

Acts of kindness
work the same.

When a buffalo sees
a dark sky lurking
on the horizon,
gathering momentum
to cross the mountain's crest,
she neither waits out
the brewing storm
nor runs the other way,
knowing the storm will catch up
then hover, an unwelcome
traveling companion.

Rather, the buffalo
charges squarely
into and through the storm
with force, shortening her
exposure to danger, while
sunlight and calm
wait to greet her
on the other side.

Seeking water
is an endless quest
for the sycamore tree,
pumping liquid
upward through root
and trunk and branch
and twig, all to nourish
the green leaves
splayed open toward
sunlight and breeze.

The leaves broaden
longer and wider,
wider and longer,
until sunlit hours shrink
and water grows elusive,
forcing the tree
to hold scarce nutrients
close to its heart,
a change in posture
from expansion.
to conservation,
a storyline shift
that transforms leaves
into colors of flame

and iron, one last
spectacular bow
to beauty
born from change,
one step nearer the
next season of abundance.

Ladybug
ravishing
in red, solo
in flight, wings
aflutter, beholden
to none. How
surprising, then,
to walk along
the stream trail,
weaving through
the redwood stand
and come upon
this ladybug
huddled among
thousands
of her kind,
a magnificent
gathering of
slick crimson coats
nestled together
for protection
and comfort
from the
winter's chill
until the days swell

with longer
light, and
the sisterhood
disperses,
each ready to fly
alone once more.

Sometimes the miracle
hides in the waiting

when all appears
still in the desert,

but wonder is at work
stringing together

a sequence of essential
acts until, all at once,

a super bloom—
a rare explosion of

wildflowers blossoming
in unison, displaying

a crush of color, a jubilee
of nature's will to grow.

The miracle opens when
autumn rain falls

and soaks deep into the soil
to reach the dormant seeds.

Too much water will
carry away the seeds,

but too little and they wither.
Then, in later winter

the earth must slowly warm
with ample cloud cover to protect

from scorching desert days
and freezing nights.

Come early spring
strong winds must calm,

offering mercy
to the young sprouts

growing tender roots.
Then, and only then,

all seasons sing
with the bursting

of countless blooms
of sunny brittlebush

and orange poppies
blanketing the arid land

in a once per decade
act of defiance

against probability,
against impatience,

against skepticism.
An offering of awe

waiting in the desert
for the patient,

the hopeful,
the resilient.

LET'S . . .

An Invitation for Togetherness

Let's rest together
in the space that separates
words, where quiet hangs
like a hammock
strung between sounds,
where silence is not
an awkward beat
but a place to breathe
in the chasm below noise.

Let's sit side by side
in the gap between
question and answer,
problem and solution,
stillness and movement,
and let's invite wisdom
to join us.

A friendship
grounded in trust
is like platinum—
precious and rare,
withstands heat,
enduring.

A friendship
rooted in loyalty
is like iron—
strong and magnetic,
pulling the compass
needle north.

But a friendship
built on gossip
is fool's gold—
shiny but lacking
and sold by hawkers
who trade in the dark
alleys of false comforts.

True friendships
are elemental.

Let's wrap each other
in slow-releasing joy,
sharing it like wild
orchid seeds that flit,
light and feathery,
unconcerned with where
or how to land.

Let's resist
the fleeting allure
of what's shiny and fast
and sink into a slow,
sustaining joy—the kind
buoyed by a quick laugh,
a quick return to gratitude,
or a quick sprint to giving.

In gratitude for
the sun
and all givers
of free light:
falling meteors,
clusters of stars,
flames of fire,
and us,
who shimmer
much the same.

Though too subtle
for the eye to see,
a faint glow
radiates from
all of us,
shining brightest
when our hearts
open widest.

Just like the stars,
we share light
without even knowing,
without even trying.

Let's walk together through
the anxious moments,
the ones that flatten
the seedlings of courage
and confidence
like a wild boar
trampling on baby
clover and sedge.

Let's build fences
around these feral
thoughts, invasive to the
delicate environment
of the mind, as they
uproot the goodness
of our inner garden,
and may we remember
these untamed brutes
have no home in us.

For some, the prayer
is in the song with
notes floating up.
For some,
it's in the words
arranged
and rearranged.
For others,
it's in the numbers
repeating, repeating,
or the colors mixed
to draw us closer.

But once answered,
the prayer for bravery
to untether and share
our inborn gifts
evolves into
a new prayer,
one of gratitude
for the soul's stretching
as it explores and shares
the inner divine.

Let's be the ones to see
rolling stones
where others see boulders,
bouquets of wild violets
where others see weeds,
abundance
where others see clutter,
a communion of friends
where others see crowds,
and loaves of sustenance
where others see crumbs.

Though overshadowed
by the dancing colors
of wax and flame,
it's the wick that's essential
to spread the candle's light.

Braid a wick too thick
and it uses extra fuel,
while a wick too fine
starves the flame.

A candle burns
cleanest and longest
when its wick
is sized just right.

What feeds the flame
impacts its brightness.

Let's scan the horizon for delight
and let sunlit particles fall on us

like grains of wild honeysuckle
pollen in early spring,

the individual granules invisible
by sight but material to growth—

gathering, collecting,
blanketing us with an

awareness that we are made
to experience this sort of grace.

If you invite me,
I'll go with you
beyond the crust of
pleasantries,
past the cautious sifting
through words
to the place
where we can sit
in what's real—
far from the self-
conscious muting
of emotions
and the burden
of what's next,
away from the
pretense of normalcy,
and just park ourselves
for a while in the soot
and grit of grief,
with time and kinship
as our salve.

Let's be the brave ones
who tread from guarded giving
into courageous generosity—
filling the need before the request,
saying yes when reason says no,
hoarding less so others have more,
trusting our future cup
will be full enough.

Use me
as a windbreak
to shelter you
from weary blows
and protect from erosion
of hope.

Let me
give you rest from
the unrelenting prairie winds
so you can experience the
rare luxury of stillness.

Let's be the ones
to flatten the horizon
when the boat's adrift,
hold the other end
of the bridge
when the footing's
unsteady, point
to the cairn when
the map's edges fade,
unfold the family quilt
when reassurance
feels far, and blow wind
into the doldrums
when the water stagnates,
onward.

Intention.
Travel back
to find Latin roots
that mean
stretch forward.
And in French,
it means *to hear.*

Such power in both—
stretching
and listening—
essential skills
for the mental resolve
to achieve.

Mere intention
can never be our sole sister
in the quest for a dream.
But it is our start.

Let's be the salt
that allows
others to float

on ocean swells,
an invisible presence
gifting buoyancy

and rest from
the dark waters
beneath.

Once I was the maker
of wind, or so you believed,
soothing with a balmy
breeze and blowing trouble
beyond the horizon.

But can you see now
I was never the one
to make still air move?
I merely stood behind
as your wind shadow
to shield you from arctic blasts
and simooms with gusts
strong enough to reshape
the dunes.

Now it's time
for you to build
your own wind shadow
to shelter yourself
and those who follow.
Then you will discover
neither you nor I
can ever be the wind.

Let's be honest
that we need grace
and ask others
to hold our faith
for us
in moments
when it feels
more burden than gift.

Yes, and let's invite
grace to hoist us
over complacency and
past what's fleeting
to where bliss waits,
arms open for us
to fully relax
into ourselves,
embodying our
own holiness.

Yes.

A day may come when
you are a monsoon

hovering over a wildfire,
killing roaring flames,

the source of urgent relief
to tall prairie grasses below

as your deluge of
selflessness saves.

But more probable:
every daybreak offers

the choice to be
the drop of dew

that nourishes a single
blade of grass each dawn

essential, but unnoticed
by all but the one,

your generosity received
drop by drop.

Let's be the
steady flame
that soothes
with its soft glow,
unwavering in
the darkest night.

Let's invite others
to gather round
our light
to share in simple
togetherness,
grateful that we've
drawn them near
to illuminate
the love we share.

Thanks for trusting me
in the dark warrens
of your sadness, allowing
me to sit next to you
through the blackened tunnels
where you retreat
to absorb the vibrations
of sorrow, beside you
until you feel ready
to make your way
back to light,
where I also will be.

Let's grab hold
of the passing breeze
like blades
of a windmill,
rising from the
grassy meadow.

Let's look
for ways
to pocket
the unseen gusts
and the gales,
embracing
not resisting,
a boundless
resource ready
to serve.

Thanks for
letting me
be the art
that hangs
a smidge off-center
on your wall,
unrestrained by the
dictates of a ruler or the
temperamental bubble
trapped inside a level.

Others have tried
to make me plumb,
but you celebrate that
straight lines
and rigid grids
are not for me.

Let's be the ones to harbor peace
and discard resentment,
offer refuge from perfection
and make room for vulnerability.

May we hold tight to mercy
and release old hurts,
be shelter from fear
and a waypoint for seekers.

Let's be a hideout
from hollowness
and a haven for expression,
a retreat from false pretenses
and a hermitage for soulful glee—
and let's leave
the window open
for breezy laughter.

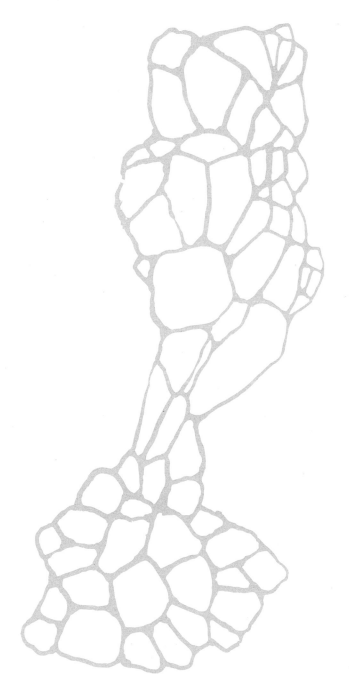

Solstice
comes from Latin
for *sun stopped*
and so may we
be still—
twice per year
come winter,
come summer—
in honor of
the year's longest
and shortest days.

May these markers
energize and renew
as the daylight
waxes and wanes
through the seasons,
always in flux,
never static,
never cowering to change.

Nature's rhythm
reminds that
time is
ever shifting,

though sometimes
so gradually
we don't notice
until the sun stops
for just a beat.

Let's be the ones
to pepper our conversations
with what's real.

What if it's our turn
to speak against
the vandals

who desecrate
goodness, the thieves
who steal optimism,

the hawkers who sell
boxes of vanity, falsely
claiming their contents

contain liberty and joy.
What if it's time
for a revival

of the basics—
of ideals that sound
soft and airy

but in their pure form
rest on character that
requires true courage

and confidence.
Could what's real be
kindness, empathy, love?

Will you please tell me
when you change?
I long to see
the you of now
but the vapors of
your younger self
cloud my perception,
leaving me to wonder
how well I know you today,
a mixture of past and future,
in flux and evolving.
It's your job to grow
and my gift to greet
you wholly, so please
don't let me miss it.

Let's release our fear
of the river's current
and our uncertainty
about when to drift
downstream,
paddle upstream,
or stand knee-deep
on the reedy
bank and wait
for rescue.

Instead, let's
embrace that
we are part of
the river too,
changing her
tempo, her flow,
her curves
by our presence,
just as she
changes us.

The well of words
runs dry
when the searing
sting of loss
burns the ground
on which we stand,
when even the most
loving language
is a weak opponent
to the strangling
heat of grief.

How I wish
my words
could be the balm
that helps your
wounds to heal,
but they
are no match
for the sadness
that suffocates
like a weighted
blanket on a hot
August night.

Even mighty words
cower at the roar
of this moment,
so instead
I offer simply
what's true:
I am here.
I am praying.

Let's visit
our inner
hermitage,
a place of stillness
where alone
is not lonely,
and unlock
the courage
to clear out
our ego
to make room
for the divine.

Let's linger
here
while our
chemistry changes
enough for
our soul
to expand
into the space
it longs to be,
grateful
for a human
home but

untethered
from our will,
now open
to the intentions
of a higher power.

Thank you for planting a
garden with me in
the dark corners of my heart
where acedia grows wild
and apprehensions multiply.

And for sharing your vision of how
lush joy will sprout here too,
though sometimes needing
a bit more care,
and for showing it's possible
to propagate the sort of bravery
that once felt as elusive
as coaxing an orchid to rebloom.

Thanks for knowing
I must tend this plot alone,
while offering the steady gift
of togetherness
and a soft clearing for solitude
to greet solitude, a place where
new perennials will soon emerge.

Let's be the ones
to see grace

wafting above hardship,
like a smoke signal

burning on the horizon,
fueled not by fear

but by mercy,
signaling the message

that even in unfamiliar lands,
hope waits for us.

Allow me
to be the
moss growing
north on your
oak tree,
a natural guide
home when no
compass points
to the trail
you wandered from,
either by
accident or intention.

And may I be
a notch in your
Orion's Belt,
three stars
evenly spaced
in the winter sky,
a celestial marker on
which you can rely?

Let's be the vessel
to collect the juice
of trust and faith,
undiluted and untainted,
then share our cup
with others
so they may taste
its natural sweetness.

I'm here
to soak with you
in the mud bath
of your sadness,
submerged under
the messy darkness,
no plan to wash
away the heartache
or pretend all is tidy
when it's not.

Let's wallow
side by side
in the muck,
knowing someday
we will rinse the
heavy away,
but not yet,
not today.

Let's be the ones
to embrace the cocktail of
knowing and unknowing,
rooted and weeded,
bedrock and apex,
boulder and feather,
doldrum and typhoon,
prime meridian and equator.

Let's trust in hope,
our patient partner,
and grace, our guide.

When the steep trail
is slicked by fallen leaves,
some hikers avalanche
their bodies downward,
forward tipping
as they go; others plod
with duck feet;
still others zigzag
to avoid a muddy tumble.

Different days
call for different ways,
shifting step by step with
the changing landscape.

It's hard,
the unknowing,
but that's no reason
to keep us from going.

Let's stand firm
like coral reef
in the life of a child,
serving as a buffer
between storm and shore,
softening the impact
of relentless waves,
creating protected lagoons
as a refuge for the defenseless,
filtering impurities,
and inviting diversity to thrive,
knowing a vibrant reef
leads to healthy oceans.

What if it's our season
to endure—*harden*
in Latin—even when
challenging
and inconvenient?

We are called to be
resolute and steadfast,
though the cells beg
for quiet and cozy,
and now is the time
to be gazelles
and outrun
the lions of
worry and burden.

Just as muscles
must tear to grow
stronger,
we must endure
before we can thrive.

Let's make quick work of worry,
the patient predator of joy,
and rest in the comfort
of being one plus one,
quirky as adjoined cherries
hanging from a single stem,
snug as a pair
of mourning doves
perched on the wire,
synchronized as two oars
pulling through placid
water, propelled
by laughter as we row.
Come giggles come.

When you're feeling short on happiness,
come borrow some from me.

When you're running low on peace,
I'm here to lend to you some.

When encouragement is what you need,
I've got some to spare.

And when love is in short supply,
let me give you more.

All expand when shared freely,
all exist to borrow and lend,
lend and borrow.

Let's
notice how
love wants
to be shared
by listening
to the buzz of
the hummingbird's
wings or the quiet
voice with bold ideas,
by savoring
the soft weave
of bamboo yarn
or the steps of a well-
worn path,
by delighting
in the earthy scent
after fall's first rain
or the rare silky halo
ringing the moon.

The current drives you
to where your feet
no longer touch the sand,
or the wind blows you
to the ragged edge of land,
or the drought leads to
a smaller harvest.

It's not how you want
it to go, and still, and still
the fireflies flash,
the moon grows full,
the shadows morph,
all priming our spirits
to stretch into the
impermanence.

It's dreamy to imagine
creativity as a trusted muse,
steady and ready
to spark agency
and to wiggle out
the next new notion
or artistic potion,
the process of creation
smooth as a glassy lake
mirroring the vision
of the mind's ideal.

But no. It's more
often like this:
a dense jungle
where quicksand
submerges
the unborn idea,
sucking it lifeless
below the surface,
trapped in the muck
of insecurity
where uncertainty
wraps itself around
young inspiration

as if a strangler vine
clutching its host tree.

It takes a
mental machete
to cut through layers
of doubt
until at last
the thick foliage
gives way
to a clearing
where the creative spirit
can stretch and move freely.

It's rare to
find the glassy lake,
but wild jungles
are beautiful too.

Let's stop hibernating,
cozy and safe,
sheltered from
what's frozen.

Could it be that now
is our spring, a time to leave
our protected caves
and attack injustice
or claw at the roots of poverty,
trusting we are strong
with a voice to be heard?

And more.
Is it time to forage
for thickets of truth
or the compassionate hives
of others also awakening
to their purpose?

Once awake,
what will lead us to roar?

Thanks for inviting me
through the back door
of your shy soul,
where you feel safe
to share the unscripted
you of birth, far from
the front steps
weathered by conformity
and the cluttered
entryway of expectations.

It's like this.

ACKNOWLEDGMENTS

Dan Ventrelle
Drew Ventrelle
Brooke Ventrelle
Ryan Ventrelle
Carolyn and Ed Harley
Laura Andes and family
Ginna Girzadas and family
Tammy Gaylord
Cynthia Leslie-Bole
Rev. John Kasper, OSFS
Alexis Orgera
Christy Mack/Bess Brand Studio

Illustrations by Hillary Waters Fayle
Book design by Shanna Compton

INDEX OF FIRST LINES

INDEX OF THEMES

ABOUT THE AUTHOR

Chrissa Harley Ventrelle braids the wild, the spiritual, and the human into poems and meditations. Her latest collection of poetry, *What Nature Knows*, focuses on the wisdom of nature and the gift of togetherness. Her first book, *May It Be: Growing a Genuine Life* (2017), offers short blessings on creating a growing, giving life.

As a writer and nonprofit executive, Chrissa has written about topics as diverse as innovations in philanthropy and the San Francisco Bay Area's best bakeries. She has a BA in Economics from the University of Notre Dame and Master's of Public Policy from the University of Michigan. Chrissa is a California native and now lives in Las Vegas, Nevada, with her husband and three kids.

www.chrissaventrelle.com
Instagram: @chrissaventrellewrites